Prince Hamlet National Park and other Literary Itineraries

Dan Williams

ISBN: 978-81-8253-967-9

First Edition: 2022
Rs. 200/-

Cyberwit.net
HIG 45 Kaushambi Kunj, Kalindipuram
Allahabad - 211011 (U.P.) India
http://www.cyberwit.net
Tel: +(91) 9415091004
E-mail: info@cyberwit.net

Printed at VCORE CONNECT LLP.

Acknowledgments

Prince Hamlet National Park first appeared in *The Raven Chronicles*, Spring 2010

I would like to acknowledge the following authors without whose help this book would have been impossible: William Shakespeare, John Steinbeck, William Coleridge, Emily Bronte, Homer, TS Eliot, F. Scot Fitzgerald, Sir Arthur Conan Doyle, Edgar Allen Poe, Arthur Miller, Mark Twain, Agatha Christie, and last but not least, L. Frank Baum. Thanks, everyone.

Preface

From my university days I've been interested in the relationship between the life found in fiction and its sometime mundane sister found in the world all around us. If normal folks were to find themselves faced with the conundrums, challenges, and especially the personalities found in the oeuvre of the works of fiction which we've known from the days of our infancy upward, how would they react? You might ask yourself, what difference does that make? To which I would answer none whatsoever, but that doesn't slake my curiosity at all.

With the price of gasoline and airline tickets and ships' passage being what it is, why not take down your favorite book or new work of fiction and insert yourself *in media res* into all that action, adventure and S*turm und Drang*. It doesn't have to be an exact match, but most of us can relate to most of the things that go on in novels, films, plays, and especially that most human of all arts, poetry. In this way a library becomes a huge travel agency without intrusive or prissy agents to bother you, and your imagination is the great machine to carry you on your travels from whatever quiet corner or noisy street café you care to open your book.

These poems, written in an epistolary or letter form which we shall call "postcards," came from just such an impulse, only instead of *reading* myself inside, I *wrote* myself inside using characters I thought would represent a wide swath of our current society and from such diversity to see how each individual would handle the iconic situations and personalities of our literary reality. These little vignettes are about correspondences and divergences and re-imaginings.

I must admit that I had 20 mini-vacations' worth of enjoyment while writing these, even hoping that the likes of Bukowski and Corso were peering over my shoulder holding forth with the kind of inebriated commentary which, I'm sure, only they could wield. Well, fellow passenger, we've stood waiting on the tarmac or the dock long enough. Come along now, think of this preface as our station. It's time we open these pages, have our tickets punched and climb aboard.

Daniel Williams

Wawona CA

May 2022

Contents

1880 New Year's Eve in the Big Tree Room

Dear Archibald and Charlotte

Here we are celebrating a new decade with some
interesting folks in Yosemite Valley
Mr. Bernard the proprietor and his wife and 3
little girls are just so nice and inviting even if
some of the adults are not so nice or inviting
I'm using a goose quill for a pen and some
black stuff scraped out of a giant sequoia for ink
Mr. Muir a Scottish gentlemen taught us how-
waterfalls and river are all singing away and we
have a nice pine log fire in the Big Tree room
There really is a big tree growing in the middle
of this room you know it takes up about half
the space the other half taken up with pioneers
and poets soldiers and Indians food and drinks
Well it started right off with Captain Boling of
the cavalry wondering if the Indians might want
to take their food and drinks outside even though
it's snowing to beat the band then the old Chief
starts up with *You and these other weenies can*
just get outta my face outta my valley and of'n
my planet Clem and I hated for this to happen
we'd just made friends with a lovely young Paiute
couple Staggering Bear and Lovely Coyote in fact
Lovely looked as though she was with child
Fortunately it was time to sit down to the buffet
I held off on the braised mutton and medallions of
meadow taking instead some rattlesnake ragout

and cheeks of rufous sided Towhee salsa George
went for a slice of badger and trout pie and soon
the table was cleared and Thomas Starr King
put up his feet and lit his pipe *Let me finish my*
bracken and blackberry salat first Jessie Fremont
cried out hanging onto her plate as if Belle Leidig
was going to attempt to wrestle it away from her
Charles Bolton saved the day by reading from his
"Poems found in a Strongbox" collection everyone
settled down to hear:

So here I've sat
while wind and rain
have set the trees a -throbbin'
waitin' on this goddamn stage
that wasn't worth the robbin'

Well that really set ol' Mark Twain Walt Whitman
and Joaquin Miller off talking trash about how modest
Bolton's ragged little lines are but how their pretension
should amuse us all when suddenly Lovely Coyote
speaks up

We have been burning in the
flames of racial intolerance
and I am with child
I must have peace
I must rest

Well Archie and Char you should've seen how Emily
Dickenson and and Mary Austen sprang up to comfort
her and take her upstairs to find a suitable bed

At ten seconds to midnight the mantle clock counted
down to 12 and we all counted with it

Happy New Year hollars John Bernard
Everybody laughs and applauds and reaches for drinks
Clem and I had it and so went upstairs to our room
in the distant east the sun arose over the breaking storm
above Half-Dome brightening the white cliff of the falls
soon could be heard down the hall the clean cry of a
newborn babe- first one for 1880- a child the color of the
earth held to its mother's breast   a child the color of hope

Char be sure to gather fresh hen's eggs day after tomorrow- when we get back to Benecia we'll make some fresh mayonnaise

See ya Soon

Clem and Maddie

A Fortnight at Musgrave Manor

Dear Derek

What a quaint old pile this turned
out to be and Geoffrey Musgrave
rather cadaverous in his smoking
jacket that really does look like it had
been smoking until the fire was put out
Brunton the butler first thing he did
was hit on me while I stepped out of
the cab "*was this the face that launched
A thousand ships?*" he mewed as he
offered me his hand I saw the maid
looked jealous so I kept my hands
to myself   first thing we did was check
out the castle keep dank and moldy
as it is and then Sherry in the library

What Sherry the laundress was doing
in the library is just one more mystery
as it happened we were there the day
that the *Musgrave Ritual* was read aloud
some old document with a lot of nonsense
about oaks and elms and numbers and such
you know me Derek if any math is involved I
throw up violently   after that Brunton was
seen pacing off steps in the master garden
but no one thought anything of it—
Brunton's about to compete in the Middlesex
Salsa Dance Off and all   but then he disappeared

just gone and that maid acting so strangely
serving us lox and cream cheese on Italian night
pouring vinegar into our wine glasses
telling us all to *'drink freely of her tears'*

Our host was very kind indeed but informed
us that since the butler had disappeared
and the maid had gone bonkers
he could no longer provide for us in his
hostelry besides he was expecting an
old school chum and some guy with a
strange name can't remember it now
starts with an "S" who just might be able
to help him get his domestic situation
back on track

Before we left the county though
we did attend the *Salsa Dance Off*—
too bad Brunton wasn't there
the prize was taken by a swivel
hipped stable boy from Brighton
toot-aloo and don't be bitch
Love

Sylvia

Aliens at the Beijing Winter Olympics

Dear Master Being Alpha 1

Just a few thoughts to apprise you of our recent
junket to Earth to participate in what is known
as *Winter Olympics* which is essentially
sliding devices on snow and ice used to travel
certain distances in the shortest length of time-
Primaat and I dressed as Swiss in lederhosen
and Tyrolean hats and waved Swiss flags when
the ancient digitally based cameras panned us
we fit in remarkably well with all the ecstatic
earthlings around us   what fun it was to see
what humans have learned to do with ice
and snow on primitive boards and blades
our Swiss contingent even invited both of us
to a luncheon to honor gold silver and bronze
as you are aware metals not seen on our world
for millennia we managed to capture one each
to bring back as souvenirs to our native world

Now comes the fun   we designed our own
2 person bobsled in sapphire blue with Swiss
insignia and ran it down the 120 meter ski jump
the crowd growing wild as we went down and down
leaving the lip of the jump we flashed into the sky
then vanished into thin air everyone straining to
see where we went and what happened to us

What happened was this- a nano second later our
wayward bobsled landed on the surface of Enceladus
Saturn's 16th moon an ice world of glorious proportions
its snow covered volcanoes belching ice instead of magma
we rode our sled down the sides of each and every one
under a sky filled with the E ring refracting sunlight into
colorful rainbows it grew late Master and we were anxious
to return home to Proxima Centauri B transforming our
bobsled back into mother ship just before take-off we
divested ourselves of lederhosen flags and Tyrolean hats

dumping them on the slopes of *Ahuna Mons*
it would have been fun to transpose into the
future just then watching as an earthling
explorer finally discovers them – can you
imagine the look on his face Master?
but we'd had enough games for one sol
can't wait for a good hyper-bath in some
glorious liquid methane CH4

Truly yours
Primaat A and Villatubolose B
Deep Space First Wing

America's Cup and the Ancient Mariner

Hey Gretchen

After the wedding we went over to Narragansett
and climbed board the *Fantasia Felice*
seemed like a great idea for a honeymoon to be
voluntary crew for a yacht in the America's Cup—
Our very first day out to sea we met one of Jerry's
cousins or something a strange old scrawny guy
with a bushy beard and a piercing right eye
he had the cutest little silver albatross on a chain
around his skinny sunburned neck and I wished
I could have one just like it but when I asked him
where he'd got it he just blanched and said

For you to wear one 'twould be absurd
For you must earn **this** sacred bird

imagine our surprise not only at his strange words
but at the way they were always spoken in rhymes
needless to say nobody talked to him very much
and he just mostly kept to himself that night we
had fried chicken for dinner provided by the
weird old salt who called himself "Scotty"

We were up against the *Cambria* and could see
her tacking on our right her masts lovely as
angels' wings and her prows high in the water—
wing-sailed catamarans are just the coolest—
for some reason they had the wind up and we

didn't and so it passed us with a woman leaning
over in our direction and saying something we
couldn't hear our boat had come to a complete
standstill in the water and it was a hellish day
and I must say our tongues were lolling like dogs
all that water and nothing to drink not even a Da Sani
after a bit we felt weak and then we felt dead and
all of us collapsed and dropped onto the deck

No fear — I'm seeing this once again
But know what to do unlike back when

All of us were struck by old Scotty's rhyme and
wondered what on earth he meant by it when he
did something really strange he dropped his silver
necklace in the sea right next to the hull of our boat

Well I must say Gretchen there was no wind but we
plowed through water like a souped-up *Glastron*
passing the *Cambria* somewhere in the blue green
waters off Newport Beach now we're all
sipping champagne out of an art deco cup

After disembarking I looked around for the
strange old salt to thank him but saw he was
busy speaking earnestly to someone in formal
wear on the dock who was trying in vain to
break away

Oh that reminds me
we've yet to return our wedding stuff to the
rental Jerry knows a sushi joint with great eels
after we ditch these wedding weeds

let's all get together for lunch
we'll invite the ancient mariner and
he can pay for it all
Bon voyage

Clarice

At the Victorian Christmas Carol Inn

Dear Taneesha

What could be whiter than a Christmas
spent in olde timey snowy olde England?
we just had to get out of Detroit this year
for one thing Buster's anger management
is getting out of hand I thought a change
of pace would do us both some good
We elected to stay at Scrooge's B&B but
there wasn't much of a bed and only warm
water and some saltines for breakfast We
tried to pin ol' Scrooge down but he just
laughed and said that was a traditional English
breakfast and after all we'd only paid 10 pounds
each for it and should be thankful we weren't in a
workhouse Buster asked Scrooge if he'd ever
enjoyed punch for Christmas I saw what was
coming and stepped between them just as
Buster was hauling off with his huge fist
Scrooge escaped a joyful punch in the mouth
We didn't get a moment's rest all night long
old Ebenezer was arguing with people in his
bedroom at least 3 of them that I counted
there were chains clanking and weird hoots
Funny thing the next morning ol' Scrooge
was a new man we had eggs and ham with
tiny delicious scones and jam for breakfast
Buster was still a little touchy though saying
as how he'd like to provide Scrooge a goose

for dinner using a fire poker and some grease
there were a couple of scrawny kids in the
breakfast room Scrooge introduced them as
"ignorance and want" Buster handed each of
them a scone saying "great names you two—
don't let me catch you near my wallet"
Christmas Day Scrooge went off to play games
and dance with his nephew and his wife
Buster and me looked at each other. Un-uh
not our kind of scene we decided to just hang out
a good thing we did for about noon along comes
this scrawny looking creature carrying a kid on
his shoulders looking for Scrooge
"Mister Scrooge said to drop by there'd be a
huge turkey here." I could see Buster begin to
seethe " Did he tell you that Turkey's name?"
scrawny guy just looked confused and said
"C'mon Tim I guess there's nothing here for us"
"Don't you see father how even nothing can be
a blessing?" the scrawny guy looked puzzled
and said "sure Tim." Buster looked at the little
fellow and said "You can't walk on your own
let alone play and run with other kids you
have no turkey for Christmas dinner your house
is probably cold and drafty and your future dim
yet you see all this as a kind of blessing?"
Tim grinned and said "bless us every one" mister
For the first time this trip I saw Buster smile
opening his fist as he reached for his wallet
"there's a poulter around the block with a huge
bird in its window Scrooge must've forgot to
purchase I want you to take this and buy it
and cook it and me and my lady will be over

for Christmas turkey dinner about 5 o'clock"
Bob the scrawny guy breaks out in this huge grin
and takes the 20 from Buster and runs off down
the street with that kid bouncing on his shoulder
When Scrooge returned we had his house all heated
with some coal we'd found and we even had a
Christmas gift for him that we'd wrapped Buster
did an excellent job of decorating the tree with a
little angel on top we told Ebenezer we're all going to
Bob's for dinner but first he must open his gift
Scrooge looked embarrassed that he had nothing for
us but tore into his one and only Christmas gift anyway
opening the box he held up a brass something that caught
the Christmas lights and threw them back into our eyes
"Well bless my soul it sure is pretty and heavy I guess
it's a paper weight for my desk" Buster held it up to
the light where you could see its wings he grinned
and growled "Humbug I tell you Humbug!"
We'll save our BarBQ for New Year's Taneesha

Buster 'n LaWanda Blevins

Occurrence in a Baltimore Boardinghouse

Dear Kevin

I thought this was a good idea
going to see the round tops at
Gettysburg staying in a cheap room
in *Baltimore* driving back and forth—
a charming woman Mrs. Clemm
and her two sweet daughters ran
the place there was a strange creature
living in a tiny garret under the roof
I'd heard Mrs. Clemm tell her daughter

'*Virginia take Eddie some of this*
sherry go on take it up to your cousin'

odd thing more than once I thought
she'd said '*husband*' instead of cousin
but that might be because I'd had some
of that excellent spirit myself she keeps
it in a cask in the basement with about
17 black cats roaming about the place

My room is next to the kitchen downstairs
one evening the wall behind my bed
began to thump as if it had its own heartbeat
in terror I ran out into the parlor only to
find Mrs. Clemm striking the kitchen wall
with a broom handle cursing
the mice that she says live there

it was then I met 'Eddie' for the first time
he had a red nose on a destroyed face
under a mane of dark hair   was
slovenly in dress and staggered a lot
I quickly excused myself to the loo
at the end of the upstairs hall
as I passed his room I was shocked
to see not only books piled everywhere
but a bust of *Pallas Athene* over the door
with of all things a huge black bird sitting
on it well I don't have to tell you the mess
that bird had made on the bust and the
floor beneath   beady eyes watched me
hurry by and it squawked once or twice—

Upon my return to the parlor I had to
introduce myself to this man in front of
Mrs. Clemm *'Hi I'm Ed Poe'* he'd said
extending a soft ink-stained hand
when I told him my name I saw a change
occur in him the likes of which
I'd never witnessed before
especially since I'd coughed into my
hankie several times due to a dry throat
he flew into a rage
Calling out *'nevermore'* and *'nevermore'*
and stomping upstairs to his room
slammed the door
I looked at Mrs. Clemm and she just
shrugged and said "*he once had a*
girlfriend"

I determined to remove myself
somewhere else that very evening
and good thing I did
I saw Mrs. Clemm and her daughters
on the street next morning
it seems a candle caught a page
of *The Humorous Torquemada*
on fire and the whole place
went up around midnight
everyone got out thank goodness
but *Eddie's* bird
they found it roasted in the ashes
of a copy of *Longfellow's Poems*
Poe himself had disappeared—
Mrs. Clemm said "he'll come back—
            he always does"
            I tell you Kev   I'm spooked
can't wait to get back to Modesto
            Fondest wishes

Yours, Lenore

Buffet at the Garden of Eatin'

Dear Ina

We'd heard about this place
how it was all-natural ambience
really reasonable at $7.99 per person
for *all you can eat* dining *al fresco*
you know me I'm used to mac 'n cheese
and boiled wieners so this was really new-
one big turn off was all the *Beware of Snakes*
signs everywhere but I guess it was a safety concern
Our Maître 'D was a young man by the name of Adam
who saw to it that we were seated comfortably telling
us all about the trees in the garden and their fruit
we thanked him grabbed our plates and began filling up
Our cashier Eve came over to explain how we may
want to try a really exotic dish that looked like applesauce
and came from the tree of (she mumbled it) "goodenevil"
honestly I only had a couple of tablespoons on my ham
but suddenly I seemed to sense a lot of stuff I didn't know
before like the two brothers working together in the kitchen
for some reason I began to realize what a terrible waste and
that one brother was going to kill the other one   I got up
marched into the kitchen and told them both to chill and
everything would be alright one of the brothers held a
knife and was busy chopping broccoli and the other
brother just laughed and told me to get out of his kitchen

We had a handsome young man who watched our table
removing empty dishes and busing them and so I said to

him "Isaac something is going to happen between you
and your dad but don't worry it'll turn out alright"
Isaac just grinned and said "he and I have had our
bad times together but nothing absolutely nothing
will cause me to not trust him completely in fact
after closing he and I are going to explore sacrificial
rock just outside the garden" I was just going to reply
when Adam with some thug he called Lucifer showed
up at our table and we were summarily kicked out of
the garden and told never to return "we just don't need
trouble makers like you in here" Adam sneered and
so we left I can tell you the only tip I left on that
table was a note that said "find another job."
Adam saw it read it and asked "well what about Job?"
I could tell that I'd tried his patience and so left
On the way out I picked some fruit off of one of the trees
and snuck it out of there I'll make a pie this weekend
and you can come over and share it with us.
Yours for wider understandings

Ruth and Esther

Cetaceans of Cannery Row

Dear Jacques

The grant money finally came through
so Dr. LeConte signed me up for a field
seminar with an old marine bio buddy of
his name of Dr. Ed Ricketts who has this
lab on the coast just north of Monterey

I set out on a far out spring day in my
rusty ol' Vee-Dub full of books and shit
a big beautiful wad of per diem in my pack
just itching to make myself one with the
consciousness of cetaceans

Dig it Jackie it was all wild mustard and
artichoke fields and then a finger of land
with blue ocean on both sides and canneries
everywhere I was to breathe salt air and fish
and formaldehyde for the next seven days

From the get go the "lab" turned out to be
this funky old house full of jars and bottles—
the jars full of invertebrates the bottles full
of beer the air full of a scratchy 78 *Parsifal*
spinning on the world's oldest turntable
the old doc himself was a friendly sort and
I thought he might be uptight until I met
his raunchy friends Mack and the boys

took me out to the beach to collect they
said they were expert at rustling frogs

When we returned from the tide pools
Doc was nowhere to be found one of
the dudes— "Hazel"— told me Doc was
over at Dora's House the "Bear Flag"
researching a paper that he was going to
call "Aspects of Mammalian Behavior"
I suggested we all plan a party for Doc
in his absence and since I'd been sleeping
in a pipe of a huge boiler out in a field I
could spend my per diem on party favors
Mack and the boys didn't think it a good
idea though he said "Doc probably
remembers the last party we threw for him"
Well Jackie this just wasn't the learning
vacation I'd wanted—no way—I mean
there was some real done stuff going
on the whole time you know suicides
and homicides and herbicides everywhere
I looked it was predator and prey out there
in a sea of troubles and all these people just
paddling to stay afloat

I just cranked my little beetle said good-bye
to the dudes and headed back to my quiet
little coma in the shady streets of Berkeley
I'd just spent a thousand bucks and nothing
to show for it—a sadder *Budweiser* man

When I got home and opened my bag to
unpack I found a brewski from Doc—
the boys had gifted me with a huge
green frog which leapt out the window
and into the iris bed   Hope to see you and
Lil at tomorrow's sit-in
Peace 'n Love

Flea

A Day at the Wizard's Amusement Park

Dear Uncle Henry

Dottie's on spring break so we went on a
lark to a place she knew from back in the day
I've got to tell you it was awesome fun— we
drove to the *Wizard's Amusement Park* just
outside Branson the first thing you do is walk
this huge cornfield maze with a Technicolor
and Dolby cyclone created by George Lucas
then you find yourself in the falling house ride
just falling until your stomach is in your mouth
and then thump someone screams and as you
step out you see a make believe body under the
corner of the deck it's just the funniest thing
but if you think that's fun it's just the beginning

From then on its one ride after another there's
the munchkins' train ride the flying monkeys'
roller coaster— 4 inversions and a 5 story drop—
the hot air balloon ride and if you're into games
there's knock the hat off the scarecrow squirt
water at the tin man and my favorite scare the
lion until he pees himself If you get hungry
there's yellow Winkies everywhere selling yellow
Twinkies and then you can do the yellow brick
cake walk or eat at Glinda's Southern Cooking

By the time you're finished with all that you still
must run through the dark wood of the Kalidahs

with trees snatching at you and these creatures
with bears' bodies and lions' heads trying to tear
you apart with their claws   it's just wonderful uncle

By that time of course you're ready for a nap
and so lie down in the field of deadly poppies—
sometime much later a munchkin awakens you
and off you go to the Emerald City Theater where
you wear 3D glasses and everything looks green

We missed the Wizard's famous magical show
    darn it   there's only one at 2 o'clock and we had
    to take Toto for his walk and clean up after him
    he's getting pretty old you know and has
    trouble chasing after monkeys flying or otherwise
    that was a bummer and we looked everywhere
    for the basketball throw so we could win prizes
    and maybe even the golden cap   if you
    get 3 baskets in a row you win the cap that
    gets you free admission next time
    but we couldn't find it anywhere on the midway
    finally we asked an old lady sweeping up with a
    broom where it might be   she pointed west
    and said "its above a sherbet shoppe just down
    the way that has a neon rainbow for a sign my
    pretties   all ye've got to do is look somewhere
    over that rainbow"

By that time Uncle Hank we were so tired we
decided to take a pass   besides we didn't like the
look of the old gal with a carrot nose and that hair
    and thought maybe she was having us on anyway

Well I've got to go now and polish my silver boots
  Dorothy sends her love   This was such great fun…
  hoping soon to have an adventure of my very own
Your loving niece

Alice

Fall Colors at the Crucible Inn

Dear Billy

Man you should see these leaves
golds and scarlets and a tint of canary
too bad Salem Mass is such a weird place
I came here for some R&R after passing
the bar and maybe a little booty with
some lovely lady leaf peepers but
was told the Prince of Peace B & B
was full up but I could get a room
at the Crucible Inn run by an old gent
name of Proctor seems I would have
to sneak out every night in order to
tom cat since Proctor demanded
everyone *say their prayers* and be
in bed *alone* by 7:00 o'clock

First night I was out on those mean
streets I ran into 4 young ladies dressed
in cloaks and they told me about a dance
being held in the forest that night one of
the ladies called herself Abigail and said
there would be a fire and lots of liquid
refreshment (she held up a sloshing kettle)
probably some quaint kind of box 'o wine

I followed them out of town to a glade
where a sister by the name of Tituba
had a fire going and was waving her arms

over it talking to herself I said "Hey sistah
what's the haps?" she just ignored me and
went for a live chicken by this time the
girls were all naked and dancing around the
fire in a circle I couldn't believe my eyes
I started to unlace my shoes and said
"Jesus" and the girl Betty dropped down in
a swoon Some old bird from town caught
us at it told us to put on our clothes and
said there would be hell to pay

Next morning I checked with Proctor at
the Inn and he said the only activity in town
would be to pray or read books with Reverend
Hale I thought I would pass on both but then he
said I could watch the witch trial if I wanted turns
out the 4 girls Abigail Betty Ruth and Mary
and the sister from Barbados were going to
be tried as witches W*itches*? Do you believe
that?

I went to Judge Danforth's office and told
him I'm a lawyer and asked him what law
had the girls broken out in the forest?
he just turned his sour old face with its
blue nose in my direction and said
"Hellfire and damnation! That's what!"

"uh excuse me" I replied "have you ever
heard of the *separation of church and state*?"

the old reprobate just laughed and said "no"

Walking back to the Inn I noticed people
were being pilloried while others threw rocks
there was a carnival feeling in the air as
gibbets were being tested in the town square
I found old Proctor in the Inn's lobby
and told him I wasn't going to wait for the
train I was out of there I paid him for one
night and asked him if I could have his
wooden name plate for a souvenir that
must've poked a sore spot cause he just
started screaming "how am I to live without
my name? I have given you my soul – *leave me*
my name" I barely heard that last part brother
I was down the road toad and gone
Yours & etc. etc.

Justin Case   Esquire

Evening Spent with Muses

Dear Ariel

Late one night came a knock upon
my door as I struggled with my poem-
I first thought it to be Edgar Allan Poe
but a glance out the window assured me he
wouldn't be driving a lemon-yellow XKE

Disgusted by the interruption I threw open
the door with bitter words and incriminations
on my lips and a frown that could melt any
ordinary classic Jaguar like butter
only to be frustrated further by an empty stoop

Hearing a giggle I spun around to find 3 women
in my room these ladies were serious partiers
Hi cutie the first one said around her gum
brushing a lock of chestnut hair back with long fingers
I'm Erato she winked *and I've brought my guitar*

Oh look you've frightened him said the second one the blonde
don't be afraid of us little man said she *and perhaps I*
Calliope will play iambs to your epic bravery on my lyre
the third lady was dressed in Hellenic tunic with bay leaves
woven into her auburn hair *I am Enterpe* said she

I just love long dreamy polymorphic flute-like descriptions-
wanting only to be left in peace I set out some dip and chips
poured some Hawaiian Punch and some pretzels and said

please allow me to finish my poem about the
Moors in Spain I just need time to focus right now

All three peered over my shoulders at the page
Oh no for pity's sake you can't use that image
look your lines are much too long – concision please
also you should try a little chiming   and so I used
short concise lines chiming and dreamy polymorphs

Finished I looked at my page wondered how did this happen?
then I heard the diminishing snarl of a lemon-yellow XKE-
Lord Byron Jones

Greek Isle Odyssey

Dear Penny

Greetings from sunny Greece
our tour boat operator-
Paulie Phemus
is a big guy with a patch over
one eye   he herds people around
as if they are just so many sheep

We set out from *Calypso's Yacht*
Harbor after drinking ourselves silly
we did stop for a whirlpool bath
at a place called *Charybdis Charlie's*   but
be careful   a swarthy little mutt
calls himself 'Mr. Scylla' will try to
get you stoned   it is well worth the
extra drachma to experience the *Sirens*
Excursion   the music almost ethereal
next to the impossibly blue sea   but it was
marred by some silly twit calls herself
Nausicaa asking everyone if she could
wash their clothes   after the performance
we berthed the boat near *Circe's Lagoon*
a fine eatery along the lines of *Hometown*
Buffet   you know what I mean   everybody
making a pig of themselves   I would advise you
to forego the cheese and the wine while there

Gosh it seems like I've been away forever
it'll be good to see Ithaca once more-
on one last fling we took Phemus out to
a place called "Sacred Cattle Steakhouse"
run by a little Greek *Mr. Helios*
but when we told the brute we had a
'Special steak just for him' Pauli just
let out a whoop and ran for his boat

Penny my love   I'll be home soon
Be sure to clean house before I get there
I hope my bow is still around the place
I feel like a little archery tell Telly
I've got a tiny toy horse just for him
    All my love
      Odie

Prince Hamlet National Park

Dear Hazel

Things are tight this year so
for vacation I stayed home and
hung out with *Hamlet* at *Elsenore*
kind of strange until I finally relaxed
and had some fun hiding behind
arrases watching for ghosts on the
ramparts at night or chatting with
this quaint old guy digging graves
in the rustic graveyard
Ophelia took me out collecting and
cataloging wild flora and then we
went for a swim in the willow pool
after snacks in *Gertrude's* kitchen
I took a nap in *Claudius's* Garden
and then enjoyed
fencing lessons with Hamlet
and *Laertes* –
just a tip though
don't drink *anything* during the sword play
and watch out for discolored blades—

Everybody hereabouts seem to be in
in mourning for a couple of students
killed on their way to England—
everyone but the prince that is—
he's a strange one
At the end of each day

I closed my eyes in a cloistered
room of quarried stone
if *Yorick* doesn't keep you up
half the night with his stand up
and infinite jests—he's a crazy man—
you can listen and just might hear
those flights of angels really
singing thee to thy rest—
For now though I've got to remember
souvenirs for everyone or as Hamlet
senior's ghost says "List List O List"
wish you were here with your bare bodkin
Sincerely yours
Stanley

High Tea with J. Alfred P

Dear Bunny

This is what I get for answering
one of those personal ads—
'*Young at heart / fond of peaches*'
I think he stretched it somewhat—
'*Skinny balding*
Dressed old fashioned with a
Stickpin " more like it

Just a bit too stiff for my liking
but there we were tromping
down the boulevards past squalid
hotels and greasy restaurants
it was getting dark when I said
'*Look here you can't we get a taxi*
or something?'
but we had arrived at the *Mermaid*
Tea Room by then really seedy
I should of thought he'd make some
small talk or ask me my sign
but he just sat turning his spoon
through his *Darjeeling* making an
annoying clicking noise with his cup

Out of sheer boredom I eavesdropped
on two old dears at the next table
one of them was going off about
Michelangelo being gay and spending

a lot of time in his studio fondling
his own work then they got up and left

I'd had enough *'Mr. Prufrock*
will you speak?' to which he merely
pointed at a dish of dainties and asked
'*do I dare to eat a peach*?'
I know these quiet types and can sense
when some perv is coming on to me
'*really sir I will not be treated in this*
abominable fashion' well then the
old trout began to throw a hissy
'I drown' he screamed *'I drown'*
well I tell you I just stuffed a scone
in each pocket and got the hell
out of there
To make matters worse
the only ride I could find back to the *Savoy*
was one of those old-fashioned carriages
with a cadaverous footman
who held the door the cheeky blighter
seemed to be snickering at me
when we'd arrived he hung around
for a tip but I put a flea in his ear
I told him to *piss off*
tell Audrey I'll be home soon
with some squished scones
Very truly yours

Fatima

Hiking Birnam Wood

Dear Lucy

At first we thought Dunsinane Air B&B
might be a great deal especially with the golf
coupon they floated to get folks to sign up
The day we arrived we were told we wouldn't
need a ride to the wood since it would come to us
The house itself is a spooky old pile haunted by
old man MacBeth who goes about using the royal we
and the old lady who constantly wrings her hands as if
she is scrubbing them but not getting them clean I gave
her some of my hand sterilizer and she seemed better after that
although I think the alcohol may have been a little rough on her
Here we were in Scotland during the autumn and you would think
we would sleep like the dead but no -people wandering about all
times of the night strident voices weeping and the old guy contending
out loud that he "kills sleep." About the third night there we heard that
the old guy's friend Duncan was murdered and that some really pissed
people were about to arrive and set things straight. There were three
lovely elderly ladies there who seemed to make everything all right
spending most of their time in the kitchen making those pots and pans
boil and bubble. We were sharing some really nice haggis with them
when they told us that MacBeth would only be slain by man "not of
woman born." That seemed pretty amazing and we thought that would
guarantee ol' MacB a long life although a sleepless one, until one of the
elderly ladies cackled and said in passing "did you know that one out of
every twenty births comes about due to caesarian section?"
Lucille by this time I just wanted to get out on the golf course sink some
holes in one but you know we never made it the whole shootin' match

was surrounded by armies whose leaders had been killed and whose wives and children had been murdered. Our last day we were trying to hump our suitcases out of there and all sorts of characters were trying to help us about half of them unsubstantial and you could see right through 'em. We should be at the Elwood P. Hankins Memorial Airfield next Tuesday about 12:45 p.m. if you wouldn't mind picking us up.

Love 'n kisses,

Hiram and Lois

The Huck Finn Resort

Dear Ralph

O sure we did all the rafting
fishing and swimming our first day out
then there was quaint ol' Hannibal—
everything sure went south after that
the whole time here our only lodging
has been a dump called
Pap's Cabins we looked forward
to an amateur theatrical the *Royal Nonesuch*
And Farmers Market as it turned out
we got some nice tomatoes and cabbages
someone had thoughtfully stacked up in back
but the *Nonesuch* itself was just some old
reprobate running around naked on the stage

There was however a nice old gal every one
called *Miss Watson* who fixed us some tea
we heard that there was going to be a chance for
some shooting on a couple of farms owned by the
Grangerfords and Shepherdsons but were horrified
to hear we'd have to decide which members of those
families we were going to shoot

I tell you Ralph I can't wait to get home
we did have some grits and hominy in a little
Café *The Duke of Bilgewater* with the
sweetest hostess you would ever want to meet
a Miss *Becky Thatcher* but I don't think

black folks are allowed in there although
Becky told us *Jim* the dishwasher is black
in fact folks were just a little too handy with
the "N" word around here for my liking

Well Ralph   I'm going to pack up and get out
will be on the 12:45 train from
Cairo I got you a souvenir just
the cutest little ol' corn cob pipe
It's yours when I get there
Yours fondly

Lydia

Iliad Idyll

Dear Herschel

We were glad to see the Turkish coast
I'll tell you it was sheer hell on that boat
then all of a sudden there's the beach
and on a sandy rise there's Troy
floating out there in the warm distance-
          all those towers without tops—

First thing we lunched at *Agamemnon's*
Mycenean BBQ on the Beach but
stay away from the beans we all came
Down with something called
'*Clytemnestra's* revenge'
those of us who could still walk
strolled up the dunes and through
the gates of the old city
a young lady was selling tickets at
the turnstile she had a name tag
that said "Dawn" and the prettiest
pink fingernail lacquer you'd
ever seen well let me tell you
did we ever meet some characters—
there was old *King Priam* with a silvery
mien of hair and his son *Paris* a slim
willowy yoga instructor his other son
was gone but nobody would talk about him
then there was a knockout by the name of *Helen*
big hair full of sunlight and her hopelessly

overweight husband *Menelaus* whose armor barely
fit him Helen had warm brown eyes and alabaster
skin 'Meanie' as everyone called her husband
was one of those jerks who thinks cruelty is sexy
finally there was *Achilles* a well-heeled young man
gave chariot rides around the walls of Troy
and led a special excursion called "sacking the
Temple of Apollo" -that was a little too rich for
my blood so I consoled myself in Priam's Garden
the old king was a bit of nut and told some real
stretchers you'd like this one Herschel he said
once he called for a legion of archers but the
messenger thought he said arches and about 400
architects showed up there were plumb-bobs
and T-squares everywhere
At night we enjoyed bonfires on the beach
everyone was talking about '2 coins for the
boatman' some boat ride excursion or other
but not for me I'd had enough of boats
now here's the strange part and you know
how I like a good mystery on Wednesday
this huge wooden horse suddenly appeared
on the deserted beach I mean no one
was around pfffffft they'd vanished as if the
mother ship had collected them all
someone told me to grab a rope and help
pull it through the gates I said 'no way Jack
I'm on vacation' once inside it sat in the
Square of Hera of course we all took snaps
funny thing though I was looking up at the
horse's tail and could've sworn I heard
someone fart and then a lot of
suppressed laughter *from inside the horse*

I was going to tell the old king
but thought better of it chalked it up to
just another flashback to the Mycenean BBQ

The next morning as we boarded our ship
there seemed to be a lot of activity in the
old town   shouts and a lot of smoke
people hurrying everywhere
we set sail and I reminded myself to write
a terse note to the tour company
this was billed as the "*Walk with Giants
Tour*" but you know   I didn't see one giant

Gather a bunch of fresh eggs and we'll
make some mayonnaise the moment
I get back
Love ya

Roz

Island Cruise on the "Ten Little Indians"

Dear Lennie

Remember how excited I was to
win 2nd prize in the Modesto Mystery
story contest for *Death at the Dealership*?
I'd gladly give it to someone else if I could
It was bad enough being on a boat
named after a child's nursery rhyme
steered by a toothless old salt
noshing a sardine sandwich the smell
of which turned the rest of us green as the
Cornish sea off Indian Island —
But then this old bloke stokes his pipe
and I've got to tell you I thought more
then once how I'd wished I could've been
out there alone— but I was stuck
the old tar wouldn't be coming back
until Monday morning and we'd all be
holed up in this ancient pile of a house
riding an island like a clam floats on a turtle

Of course it starts to rain just as we all introduce
ourselves and the butler brought out a party record—
some silly thing about "crimes" we were all supposed
to have committed there was the most adorable
ceramic centerpiece of 10 little dancing Indians but shortly
after the Russian Prince choked himself at the piano some
fool broke it and only 9 were left I thought
whoa! This is turning into one of those mystery weekends
over the next day and night I gotta tell you people were

disappearing left and right   then the butler's wife died
talk about your wet blanket   nothing but fog outside
and not enough people left inside to play bridge

Sunday morning came and there was
just a couple of us left a Miss Claythorn and a handsome
young man looked like Geroge Clooney and the old judge
well I'm almost shocked to tell you what happened next
the young couple were playing with a gun out on the beach
and George Clooney fell down and played dead Miss
Claythorn went inside and told the old judge and he was
so broken up over the young man's death (I know what you're
thinking Len but it wasn't *that way* at all) he took
arsenic in his scotch and soda I tried to stop him   tell
him it was all a joke but too late   he heard his eyes
grew huge and then he gurgled and keeled over
It was later we found this lovely hanging
macramé woven out of sisal and bowline knots—
that the thoughtful old dear had made for us
I grabbed that and the cute little ceramic piece
of the little Indians dancing 'though some fool
managed to bust off all 10 of 'em leaving me a
ceramic ring with their poor little feet attached
but you know me Lenny   a souvenir is a souvenir

Can't guess how all the others got to the mainland
but you'd better believe that young couple and I
caught that boat come Monday morning and we
were outta there can't wait to get home to hear
my adorable little Agatha kitty purr just for me
Kind regards

Myrtle

Little Theater with Godot

Dear Myra

I thought it might be fun this little theater group
I joined you know thought it could help me
visualize and create and express more vividly
the Word of the Lord an evangelical minister's
livelihood depends on making the Word come
out right in a powerful and spiritual manner but
I never reckoned on this I showed up at this
putrid little brick building down near the skid row
mission where I sometimes testify to the drunken
insane sinners of this world and entered by a
back stage door there I was on those lit boards
with two goofy characters by the name of Didi
and Gogo and their friends Pozzo and Lucky
and this miserable looking little dried up tree
I think there was watchers in the audience
But couldn't tell for sure because of the lights
In my eyes so I says, "Howdy, I'm the Very Reverend
Billy Bones, and I've come to give you everlastin'
Life" The two bums just look at each other
exchange hats take off their boots offer me a turnip
look at their watches and say in unison "we're accursed"
well Myra, I turned down that turnip since you don't
want to be acceptin' root crops from the devil then
they asked me somethin' really strange they said
"Very Reverend Billy is your last name Godot?"
to which I says no there ain't been no frogs in this
here family tree the name's Bones B-O-N-E-S

one of the little guys Gogo I think pulls out some
chicken bones he's got in his pocket and asks if I'm
hungry   well I knew then that these guys are one
taco shy a combo plate and I became very sure
when Pozzo tries to lasso me with a rope and
ride me around the stage like a horse I made
the sign of the cross with my fingers and told him
to back off   to save the situation with grace I said
"that little tree there reminds me of the tree of
Calvary where the Lord died to save us from our
sins" Didi says "waiting must be some kind of
sin too…when may we die?" then both of them
yahoos try to hang themselves on that little tree
wrapping ol' Pozzo's rope around their necks
but that rotten old rope just snaps and they fall
in a heap I can tell you Myra I'd just about had
it then and was lookin' for a way out but all the
exit signs were missin' are without a bulb or
somethin' so I asked the audience has anyone
got a bulb? And ol' Pozzo says to me "how
many surrealists does it take to change a bulb?"
I says "how many?" and he says "two – one to
grasp the bulb while the world unscrews itself
and one to grasp the bulb while the world
screws itself" I began to pray and dropped to
my knees hopin' for guidance from above
Didi says to me "what's wrong with letting the
Light bulb rebirth itself….we can sure use a
Born again light bulb right now but the trouble
Is the long wait all we do is wait and wait and.."
Please Myra come and get me   I can't find my way
Out of here….just go to the rescue mission
Turn right and look for this putrid little brick

building whatever you do Do Not enter by way
of the back stage door
Yours in constant hope and expectation

The Very Reverend Billy Bones

Nothing Doing with the Dharma Bums

Dear Monty

Such a tacky vacation but first let me
tell you I've some exciting news for
your *mater* and *pater's* portfolio it
looks as if tobacco's oriental markets
are the Khan's lost gold mines as well
as those sub-prime loans they financed
I should think that you and Zoe will be
celebrating at the family's Newport
manse I've got my bling so no thanks
necessary Monty I'm honored to be their
broker Now to that wretched Sierra
Nevada scam I fell prey to I decided
to take my new Mercedes G for a spin
and saw an ad in *Sunrise Magazine* —
mountain climbing and hiking and a lot
of stuff about losing one's self in a pine
forest or a fragrant meadow under stars
I got to Berkeley late morning grabbed
my duck down bag and North Face pack
and got into this crappy *Ford Econoline*
van with a sequoia and a Buddha painted
on its ass-end away we went in a cloud
of burnt oil smoke just me and two guys
I was wearing *LLBean* and new *Vasques*
the two guys my "hosts" in ripped denim
faded fleece and do rags stopped us in
Turlock for some lunch which I bought

all they had was salami and cheddar and
peanuts which was "left over from last time"
Of course the Ford wouldn't start so
I volunteered the Mercedes as long as I was
designated driver while we waited for some
guy called "Alvah" to drive the G to us I got
To know my companions Ray and Japhy
Who call each other "Bhikkus" and practice
"do nothing" while riding the rails trekking
or spending time as lookouts on fire towers
I went over some of my accounts on the PDA
while they perched in full lotus position next
to the 560 highway practicing "serenity"—
"emptiness is discrimination" said Ray
"ecstasy is autos in rainbow colors" said Japhy
"Oh Damn!" said I looking at the S&P index
Then Alvah arrived in my Mercedes G
he's a swarthy little mutt with a bushy beard
as he handed me the keys he said "Grasp
these keys along with life's sweet sadness
I commend you to a world where no
matter what starts everything ends in tears"
Then we drove following the signs to
Yosemite my companions sniffing at the
new car smell of course I paid the ranger
20 bucks at the gate while Ray made a big
deal about searching his pack for money
we drove through a stone archway into
a valley of incredible beauty and wonder
we climbed a steep trail that led to two
waterfalls climbing lichen splotched steps
alongside a chasm with rainbows spanning
from one side to the other "Wow!" said Ray

"Hoo!" said Japhy "Can we rest?" I panted
Japhy ran up the trail ahead of us and Ray
took my hand helping me on the mist slick
steps Ray told me he's a writer and normally
writes about this stuff but has run dry of late
That night after an intense sunset on all the
peaks we built a ring fire the boys began to
dance around the stones and flames saying
"C'mon little lady Get nekkid with us!"
I told them "no way —get your pants on"
Next morning we made our run on Half Dome
straight up through trees then onto the shoulder
up 900 feet of semi-vertical cable and out onto
the broad granite curve that is the top Ray
began to jot notes on his pad Japhy stood on
the very edge with the valley 3000 feet below
and hollered "Hoo!" I swear Clay that salami
cheddar cheese and peanuts tasted pretty good
in a place like that the two Bhikkus chanting
facing west sitting on the rim of the world
later we climbed back down and made a camp
in Little Yosemite Valley next to the river our
flames caught the eye of a Ranger who asked
to see our permit Ray made a great show of
looking for it in his pack but wouldn't you
know he hadn't bothered getting one so we
were cited had to put out our fire and stumble
down that waterfall trail in semi-darkness with

Ray apologizing and telling me its all a
trick of the mind and not real anyway and
Japhy way ahead waving a tiny flashlight about
and hollering "Hoo!" the Bhikkus wanted to

spend the night along the road somewhere but
I'd had enough I just kept driving and we
pulled into Berkeley just before sunrise Japhy
leapt out of the Mercedes and began unloading
his gear Ray was still going on about his writing
and how he just couldn't find his grand subject
I just pointed at the passenger door and said
"You know what? Just hit the road Jack!"
he was instantly silent and began to look at me
with a strange look in his eyes as he got out he
tried to kiss my hand but I just pulled it away
"Namaste" he said and asked if I would join him
in some chai I said no of course not told them I
was going to cancel my check and got the hell
out of there Japhy had told me about the
Chinese Book of Changes and I guess it pertains
to a lot of stuff in the cosmos but not at all
to that dirty flat filthy LA. Well Monty I'll see you
at the sub-prime loan hearings and I know
where we can pick up quick cash flipping
foreclosures guess I'm going to cancel my
subscription to *Sunrise*
Namaste

Eris

Summer Soiree with Puck and Bottom

Dear Ralph and Edna

At first we thought we'd shine it on but how often
does a person get a chance to attend a Duke and
Queen's wedding the invitation appeared like
magic one morning on our dressing table its
envelope full of golden dust and it said that
one Theseus and one Hippolyta request the
honor of our presence at their July nuptials
Theseus met us at the door of his quaint castle
in the middle of a wood not far from Athens
soon we were immersed in the preparations
making cakes sorting flowers setting out wine
it was a gorgeous setting for a wedding and the
entire village was in a dither four young people
were also getting married and so family and
friends were everywhere George and I felt
just a little out of place in our rented formal
wear but Hippolyta the bride a very tall stately
lady smiled and made us feel right at home
and a good thing too some old guy called Egeus
strolled about demanding that his daughter
'sing faint hymns to the chill fruitless moon'
I asked his daughter Hermia ' is your dad alright?
he's a little bit mental isn't he?' She just winked
and replied 'you know what they say about the
course of true love' George up and says 'I think
he's some kinda nut you ask me' Well it turns
out that some of the tradesmen are going to put

on a play led by Nick Bottom a leader of the local
drama society so for fun we went out to watch them
rehearse It was dark in that forest but so help me
Edna there was light everywhere don't ask me where
it came from but we were given light refreshments
by some pretty young girls with hippie names you
know *cobweb peaseblossom mote and mustardseed*
next thing we know we're waking up and Bottom's
stumbling about asking us if we've a "pottle of hay"
Ol' George just steps right up and says 'what are you
some kinda nut?' Bottom just laughs with a curious
bray and so I says "don't be such an ass"
well as it turns out the play was a typical botch up as
you'd expect from a bunch of "rude mechanicals"

But something was going on that we were
Unaware of everybody seemed to be falling
in love with everybody else the four young
folks were switching as they are want to do
I must say I even had unforgiveable feelings
toward Francis Flute a cute little bellows mender
with a Don Johnson 5 o'clock shadow but it
all came to a halt when I saw that a strange
creature with pointy ears called himself Robin
Goodfellow was making eyes at my George
But good ol George said 'you must think I'm
some kinda nut who'll change a dove for a raven
get the hell out' Goodfellow who styles himself
as 'Puck' one of those one name rock stars I
suppose turns to the Duke and says 'lord what
fools these mortals be' You won't believe this
but at that moment the Duke cast a fish eye
upon us and says to Puck 'who invited them?'

'they were on the A list given me by Oberon
King of shadows' came the little guy's reply
'and as you can see sire he's as perfect a
gentleman as can be seen on a summer's day
but she's very common' the duke turns to us
and says, 'who art thou?' I say in a smart aleck
voice 'alack a day we art June and George Blevins'
The duke grabs Puck by his Armani shirt and says
'you fool you were supposed to invite Juno
gorgeous queen of the heavens – Oberon is going
to hear of this yet another of your Puck ups'
Georgie takes me by the arm and says 'prithee
lady let's get thee hence away from these
faeries fools and sluts 'cause far as I'm
concerned there *all of 'em* some kinda nuts'
Edna tell Ralph that we're going to get together
for bridge on Wednesday next but first I've
got to run by Gottschalks and cancel that toaster
I'd gotten on the bridal registry for Theseus
and Hippolyta Ta Ta

See you soon
Junie and Georgie

Weekend at Baskerville Hall

Dear Horace

This place is positively eerie
        although pet friendly
and it doesn't help that at midnight
the butler and his wife put on a
light show burning candles at the
upstairs window
we kept hearing of the *curse* of
Baskerville Hall but little thought
it meant the mean spirited old fart
Mr. Franklin who went about
saying '*damn the goddamn fog*'
'*damn my arthritic knee*' and the like
the moor itself with its Paleo ruins
was very interesting and we did
hike about with the knowledgeable
Mr. Stapleton and his charming sister
who explained that the curious howl
we kept experiencing was '*just the*
wind or perhaps a bittern booming'
I think he was having us on
every time he said it he looked sly
and winked at his sis
frankly it sounded like a bitch
in heat to me but what do I know
when Dr. Mortimer from across the way
dropped by to say there was a
serial killer loose out on the moor

a foot fetishist who steals people's boots
that was the final straw – having just one boot
that and the two guys from London
who showed up just as I was
hustling my suitcase out the front
both of them smoking smelly pipes
indoors no less
I cursed them both in passing and
asked the universe what kind of
moron goes about befouling the air
we must all breathe
the skinny one in the deerstalker
with the meerschaum thought
himself a wiseguy I guess I heard him

turn to fatso and say

'*Elementary*'
I lost it then   gesturing with my finger
'*O yeah   elementary this*'
not one of my finer moments
I can assure you
can't wait to get home to the cats
        have had my fill of dogs and fog
Cheers!

Melinda

West Egg House Party

Howdy Rae Ann

Well the kids went an' got me this here
trip to take a look at some o' these here
mansions that the rich folk hereabouts
call home   damned if I don't wish they'd
saved their money This young kid Nick
meets me at the train and he talks funny
keeps sayin' a boat instead of *about*
ya' know like his people are all from up
north somewheres   well says I lets get goin'
with this culture stuff so I can get back
to my okra and taters an' he turns to me
an' says- as god is my witness- "Let's go get
crazy with Jay 'n Daisy" So we drive over
to this place with the stupid name o'
West Egg and I says *I'll take mine over easy*
and the kid just looks kinda goofy at me
and turns into this driveway long as the
Virgina Pike leading up to this castle with
those pointy windows and I say "we goin'
to church here?" The boy just laughs and
opens this fancy door big as a barn and
there we are right smack dab in the middle
of the most gosh durned party you could
ever imagine big ol' cars with hood ornaments
like chrome statues and women of every kind
dressed up like fur bearin' critters and them
wanting to put water in my whiskey and all
(what the hell's the matter with 'em)

Well the shindig lasted until the rooster crowed
I was half asleep when this gal Myrtle comes
over to me with those big goo-goo eyes and
hits on me giving me the ol' come hither—
"no way" says I I wouldn't mess with her
even if she didn't have that big bandage on
her nose and a brute of a guy watching
her every move "Who's that?" I says to Nick
and point at the big guy "Oh that's
George her husband" he says and I say back
"Well guess what— ol' George's got a gat in his
pocket" "Oh don't be silly, old sport" says
this young guy with a big toothy grin and
patent leather hair "O Woody, I want
you to meet Jay Gatsby this is his party"
Nick says I take the guy's scrawny hand
and pump it "Mister Gatsby this is great
just great I say" "Let me freshen your
drink old sport" he says pouring
some kind of hooch out of a pitcher
"You shore have plenty o' that stuff"
says I and it kinda tastes homemade
if you get m' drift" I winked at him
but Gatsby just smiled and said "don't
be silly old sport" He takes me by the
shoulder and we walk out on the porch
over the water I don't mind telling you
I was just a little uncomfortable standin'
out there next to this guy in the dark
the only thing I could see was his teeth
'cause he smiled all the time and way off
in the distance this itty bitty green light
Gatsby stopped smiling suddenly and says

"You know Woody... tender is the night"
I didn't know what th'hell he meant but
I was a little spooked by then I tried to
lighten things up a bit "Well Jay I don't
know about the night but that's the way
I enjoy my rib eye steaks" then I noticed
him a starin' at that green light way off
and I says "Lissen Jay my ol' pap once
told me somethin' I'll never forget he
knew that the future was a gonna change
things especially cause there was gonna
be stop lights in all the crossroads at
Coon Corners where we lived...now you
see that green light? He told me whenever
you see a green light from now on son
you just go like a sonuvabitch you just GO
and so Jay I'm a tellin' you to jus' look at
that teeny green light aint it cute? and do
what it's a tellin' you to do" "I guess I will
old sport" he says and so I go grab Nick
and tell him I've had enough I got on
the train that very night and was back to
Missoura in a shake of a lamb's tail
Thanks for the homemade mayonnaise
Rae-Rae I had me some deviled eggs
first thing I got back home
Your ol' buddy
Elwood

Postcard from Wuthering Heights B&B

Dear Larry

I swear you'd love this guy
our innkeeper with haunted looks
this *Heathcliff* -something of the gypsy
about him- what a way to greet your
guests— he actually said '*we get so few*
visitors here I hardly know how to act'
but ah the Yorkshire moor - first day out
we raced our ponies to the barn - leapt
stone fences wind in the heather
blue skies singing larks and *last one*
there to be the slave of the other
that was Heathcliff's idea what a strange
bird he is next day he took us to a
lovely old stone crag he called *the castle*
-Heathcliff pacing back and forth
as though expecting someone-
there was something whimsical about him
even though he could have used a bath

Thank God some neighbors the *Littons*
had an old-fashioned fancy dress ball
in the "Grange" next door
I danced my first cotillion — weird
Heathcliff peering through a window—
we took a break at *Henley's Tavern*
a fine old place to toss back a pint

I tell you Larry this is one
depressing dump I'll be happy to
blow this place for *Boise*
the only two women around here
are Ellen the housekeeper and
Isabella a pathetic scullery maid creature
it was truly strange when upon departing
I thanked *Mr. Heathcliff* for his hospitality
he just stared off into the distance
and said of all things *call me Cathy—*
    warm up the tube bubba I've gotta
    catch up on my *Twin Peaks*
                    Fondly yours

    Flo

www.ingramcontent.com/pod-product-compliance
Lightning Source LLC
Chambersburg PA
CBHW022202160726
48282CB00024B/298
9788182539679